A Book of Verses

Johanna Pang

A Book of Verses

Editing, typesetting, and illustrations by Johanna Pang

First Printing, 2023

ISBN print: 978-1-7348535-8-2
ISBN e-book: 978-1-7348535-7-5

With love for the Lord
and gratitude for Jeremiah

Foreword from the Author

Almost one third of the Bible is written in poetic verse, which I believe attests to poetry's ability to simultaneously share and evoke subliminal experience. While already an internal processor, the onset of the COVID-19 pandemic provided me with additional time to indulge in personal reflection. One particular morning, I was deeply struck by the wild, intense scene of Exodus 32, when Moses returns from Mount Sinai to find God's people bowing down to the golden calf. I was moved to write a poem, to seek a medium that would help me meditate on and internalize how this scene must have looked, felt, and sounded. I wanted to immerse myself in the verses by writing my own poetic reflections. I find that imitating the style of scripture in writing helps me to connect with it in new ways, and that is the ultimate goal I set for this book.

I cannot boast of impressive poetry. Rather, what I hope to inspire in whoever may pick up this small collection of verses is the desire to meditate on scripture through poetry. Writing helps the mind connect with ideas in deeper, unutterable ways, and I want to encourage you, the reader, to engage in this medium we have been given. Revelations do not have to be these impressive, unprecedented ideas. They can just as readily be birthed by reiterations of a known idea by introducing new angles and dimensions that enrich personal reflection.

For each poem in this book, there first appears the Bible verse that inspired it, with scripture quotations from The ESV® Bible (The Holy Bible, English Standard Version®), copyright © 2001 by Crossway, a publishing ministry of Good News Publishers. The poems are by no means meant to summarize or explain the Bible verses—they are merely my own reflections on what resonated with me in a particular reading. With that being said, each verse comes from a full book within the Bible that has its own context, and the reader should always keep this in mind. In all of God's works, there is a delicate balance, and we should strive to maintain that balance in our understanding.

Meditations on...

Romans 8:26

"*Likewise the Spirit helps us in our weakness. For we do not know what to pray for as we ought, but the Spirit himself intercedes for us with groanings too deep for words.*"

A thousand verses and two thousand adjectives I could pen,
but I have found that all pales in comparison
to those sublime moments
where all words seem unfit—
for what can mere marks of man do
but to the awe of God submit?

When I am seized by the arms of purest joy
and bestowed a glimpse of nature's graces;
or when I am weighted down by chains of sorrow
and all but succumb to the torments of shame,
words my mind could never fathom,
that my lips would fail to speak—
unto the Spirit I relinquish the burden of speech—
may He sing and cry out for me.

Ephesians 3:17-19

"so that Christ may dwell in your hearts through faith—that you, being rooted and grounded in love, may have strength to comprehend with all the saints what is the breadth and length and height and depth, and to know the love of Christ that surpasses knowledge, that you may be filled with all the fullness of God."

From seed to sleep
will I breathe life into its air,
and every threat it faces,
I too, shall assume to bear.
Against the world I will shield it—
the stinging of the frost,
the beating of the Sun—
my hands shall be the walls
which guard my little one.

It shall be planted by a love so sure,
that even the angry, howling winds
could not uproot its grounding, so secure.
It shall weather well the storms that pass,
and all the while, I shall prune it
to save it from the excess that would only weigh its body down,
and save it from the death within itself.

My pain will be to see it shaken,
but how much greater
my joy will be to watch it grow,
bearing the fruits
of that love which first bore it.

*"Now to him who is able to do far more abundantly than all that we ask or think,
according to the power at work within us,"*

You bring possibility into existence.
Even as one who dwells in that house,
this meager poet could not pen such intricate creations nor narratives as you:
out of darkness you drew the earth and it became,
this earth which teems with life where no two are exactly alike,
and every kind is sculpted according to unique design.
Then there is that awesome tale,
written through centuries and across generations,
where the enemy's greatest triumph
became his greatest defeat;
where the fall of the first of us
led to the redemption of us all.

"For we are his workmanship,* created in Christ Jesus for good works, which God prepared beforehand, that we should walk in them."

We are each a poem—
angled reflections of God.
We are each His poem.

* *The Greek word for "workmanship" is* poeima, *meaning "something that is made"* *"that this is God, our God forever and ever. He will guide us forever."*

He will guide us wherever we go—
in rightful war, He is our greatest strength,
the ally king who brings triumph to the faithful;
in darkness, He is our enduring light,
our hope in the Son never ceases;
in trials, He is our boundless joy,
the Spirit fills us with His good graces;
in the unknown, He is our certainty,
where we are blind, He sees it all;
He will guide us everywhere we go.

Exodus 3:14-16

"God said to Moses, 'I AM WHO I AM.' And he said, 'Say this to the people of Israel: "I AM has sent me to you."' God also said to Moses, 'Say this to the people of Israel: "The LORD, the God of your fathers, the God of Abraham, the God of Isaac, and the God of Jacob, has sent me to you." This is my name forever, and thus I am to be remembered throughout all generations.'"

You were content to dwell in a tent.

You were content to leave our faulty memories without a face to remember.
Instead, you came as wind and fire and breath and other special common things.

You were content to be loved by people who would forget you until they needed you,
to be a father to children who would walk away from their heritage,
to be seen in all things yet never fully seen.

"And you were dead in the trespasses and sins in which you once walked, following the course of this world, following the prince of the power of the air, the spirit that is now at work in the sons of disobedience—among whom we all once lived in the passions of our flesh, carrying out the desires of the body and the mind, and were by nature children of wrath, like the rest of mankind."

He who first rebelled orchestrates winds of malintent
against the voice of God.
Directing belligerent squalls,
he distracts with mayhem and malice
and cues the entrance of malady and misery.

But under hushed winds he whispers
his ultimate deception: sovereignty.
With a soft breeze he coaxes man
to become his own master
and lean into crooked winds.

Swept away by a howling gale,
the fool trumpets his own authority.
Giving in to every proclivity,
he is blinded from the truth:
he does not lead himself, but follows
the conduct of the enemy as he joins the chaotic ensemble.

Psalm 106:19-20

"They made a calf in Horeb and worshipped a metal image.
They exchanged the glory of God for the image of an ox that eats grass."

From the fire it was born,
and slaughtered by the blaze it would be,
once its bright-eyed luster stare
turned tarnished and dull.
Every pretending god may well be
an ox that eats grass.

When the people were made to drink
the golden ashes of their god,
what would they recall?
Did the lifeless beast ever yield
any reward for all the gold it demanded?
Did it ever do anything
but return a bovine stare?
I will look to the living God,
while every pretender may well be an ox
that eats grass.

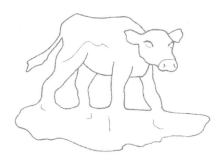

Exodus 32:17-19

"When Joshua heard the noise of the people as they shouted, he said to Moses, 'There is a noise of war in the camp.' But he said, 'It is not the sound of shouting for victory, or the sound of the cry of defeat, but the sound of singing that I hear.' And as soon as he came near the camp and saw the calf and the dancing, Moses' anger burned hot, and he threw the tablets out of his hands and broke them at the foot of the mountain."

How twisted are the melodies of the wicked,
the chanting of men bewitched by worldly gold.
Under the haze of demonic glee, forgotten was the sound of holy reverence—
there was no victory, there was no grief, there was no God.

Psalm 18:28

"For it is you who light my lamp; the LORD *my God lightens my darkness."*

As night consumes the warming sun
and dim stars remain,
the earthen lamp flickers out
and coldness makes its stay.

With shadows' borders now erased,
the darkness only I see
and everywhere the fumes of fear—
nowhere the light I need.

In my despair I cry for strength
and sight for unseeing eyes.
In silent stillness I sit and wait—
and it is then, that I see

The light does not leave me,
even in the darkest hour of the night.
I look up to see not a dark void, but stars amidst a violet sky
and the moon echoing the sun's promise to return.

A wondrous whisper of promised light
blooms within the heart—
the dwelling place of the Holy Spirit
whose fuel shall never exhaust.

Against a darkened world it shines
intense and bright as Sol;
darkness and all its spawn recede
back to the depths of Sheol.

A thousand hearths it spreads to warm—
that humble little flame;
so long as faithful hope abounds,
evil shall be dismayed.

"But let justice roll down like waters, and righteousness like an ever-flowing stream."

When justice storms with its deafening roar and writhing waters,
where will I find refuge?
In the midst of a torrent
the righteous one finds shelter in the ways of God,
with honesty as his brace,
humility as his covering,
and compassion as his all-embracing foundation.
In the night he sits to rest
and on his refuge he leans,
unmovable like mountains.
He sleeps peacefully and holds confidence
in the integrity of the Lord's walls.

But the ferocious flood engulfs the fool
who fumbles with what he has.
He stands tall, but with no footing
he sinks in floods of unbelief—
in desperation he throws up his tarp of pride
but the rolling waters drag him under as
he chokes on his own deceit—

in the cold, silent darkness,
he curses his crooked lean-to which broke
down in the wake of judgment.

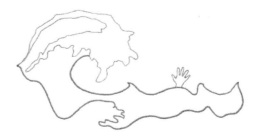

*"But the L*ORD *of hosts is exalted in justice, and the Holy God shows himself holy in righteousness."*

He sits upon His holy throne, the Holy One,
in his court of divine justice.
The brilliance of truth radiates about Him;
His holy righteousness pervades the room.
In the moment He so desires,
His omniscience knows
the truth and deceit of all;
not limited by the eyes of man,
which forever prove short-sighted.
He wields a faultless discernment.

Oh! How glorious to be judged by the One most righteous
who has lived the way we ought but do not;
the human judge fails to keep to his own word,
but the Almighty God is forever faithful.
He fears no man—
no man can make Him bend
to a wicked will,
for He tolerates no wickedness in His court;
the Son is the jury who sits at His right hand,
the Spirit a witness.

Oh! He is the perfect model of justice:
He does not sentence with any hesitation in His heart;
He arrives to His verdict of truth
from a means free of malice and grudges;
He is not bound by the human law which fails
to protect the innocent and offer guidance in extremity,
for He Himself commands complete law;
He does not fear to convict the wealthy official,
for no one can deny Him his title:
The Most High God, The Lord our Righteousness.

Isaiah 29:5-6

"But the multitude of your foreign foes shall be like small dust, and the multitude of the ruthless like passing chaff. And in an instant, suddenly, you will be visited by the LORD of hosts with thunder and with earthquake and great noise, with whirlwind and tempest, and the flame of a devouring fire."

The Lord of Armies stands above,
all tremble before His unequalled might.
The fullness of His glory shames
man's greatest warriors—of reality and mythology—
there is no more magnificent sight.

There is no steed swifter than His holy mount,
no escaping his unwavering pursuit.
Clothed in robes of righteousness,
His wrath hurtles toward His enemies in fearsome glory
with a brilliance greater than that of the Sun.

No one, nor all, could stand against the sword of His mouth
which slays wickedness with sharpest judgment;
with a mere whisper He summons eager armies,
the winds are directed by His will;
His voice shakes the rock beneath the enemy's feet;
in His hands He wields burning flames and drowning waves;
Heaven and Earth await His command.

"At that time Joshua spoke to the LORD in the day when the LORD gave the Amorites over to the sons of Israel, and he said in the sight of Israel, 'Sun, stand still at Gibeon, and moon, in the Valley of Aijalon.' And the sun stood still, and the moon stopped, until the nation took vengeance on their enemies. Is this not written in the Book of Jashar? The sun stopped in the midst of heaven and did not hurry to set for about a whole day."

The skies were stilled—its moon and stars and sun—
while brighter burned the wrath of God.
Amidst a loud and raucous heat, nations warred and bled,
and the armies of cities idolatrous and wicked,
scorched by righteous fury,
perished.

Hebrews 1:3-4

"He [Jesus] is the radiance of the glory of God and the exact imprint of his nature, and he upholds the universe by the word of his power. After making purification for sins, he sat down at the right hand of the Majesty on high, having become as much superior to angels as the name he has inherited is more excellent than theirs."

Jesus sits enthroned above;
Michael, Gabriel, Raphael and Uriel—
all herald His name.
He is superior to all the angels,
among whom even the evil one, once was named.
The prince of lies deceives himself
by assuming a rival in Christ.

See how the light forces the darkness to shrink back
into its sulky recesses.
It is the Sun that allows night to enter,
and reach as far as it may;
but when that first ray of light enters,
and touches the ceiling of the world,
how quickly darkness withers
where light begins to bloom.

Defined by the absence of light, darkness is.
Confined to the shadows,
it clings to brightness' edge—
a perfectly litotical existence.
But the light is an independent hope,
a flame that the darkness could never hope to swallow.
Nurturing, attractive, brilliant and warm,
superior to the darkness, the light is.

"*For there is no truth in their mouth; their inmost self is destruction;*
their throat is an open grave; they flatter with their tongue."

Tongues of snakes drip flattery and falsehood;
they swing wild without control
like the body which bangs against the bell's acoustic bulge
with its boisterous tone and loud repercussions.

Such tongued rebellion burns like fanned tongues of flames
and swallows falsities
to patronize a deeper grave.

This tangled and twisted maze of lies
shall the disoriented snake confound,
whose throat shall welcome his own deceit
and stomach his own demise.

"For you shall be like an oak whose leaf withers, and like a garden without water.
And the strong shall become tinder, and his work a spark,
and both of them shall burn together, with none to quench them."

The mighty oak watched, every day,
as the river passed it by.
It knew of others who drew life from the river's swells,
but instead, from the world, it chose to draw strength.
Slowly, its soul began to dry.

Roots withered first, and the oak lost its grounding.
It swayed easily to the winds of the West and became prone to evil's slightest breath.
Once, it heard the faintest whisper on a wind,
"Lean to me and you shall be given strength,"
but the foolish oak declined.

Body was next consumed by the creeping drought.
The trunk, once mightier than a hundred men, now whittled down to the meagerness
of a twig.
Again, it heard a voice,
"Draw near to me, and you shall be healed,"
but the proud oak resisted.

Arms the tree could no longer hold began to quiver, bend, then break.
It was impossible to support such burdensome life alone, and the oak grew weary.
Once more, it heard a cry from the river,
"I am here, you need do nothing but come!"
but the stubborn oak refused.

Leaves that had once breathed life fell amongst deadened roots.
As its hand fell to strike the ground,
a spark ignited and the mighty oak set itself ablaze.
The oak writhed in agony as its armor shriveled to ash,
and the river wept as it was blinded by burning light.

"Bring no more vain offerings; incense is an abomination to me.
New moon and Sabbath and the calling of convocations—I cannot endure iniquity and
solemn assembly.
Your new moons and your appointed feasts my soul hates;
they have become a burden to me; I am weary of bearing them.
When you spread out your hands, I will hide my eyes from you;
even though you make many prayers, I will not listen; your hands are full of blood."

The God whose judgment struck down nations—
who brought proud Egypt and Assyria to their knees—
whose mere whistle summoned armies—
whose wave of the hand stays the roaring waves of the sea—

The same God of wisdom and peace—
of righteousness and justice,
eternity and strength,
the same God's heart grows weary—
not from the burden of judgment, nor of provision,
but of iniquity and empty offerings.

On the prescribed day, you celebrate the Lord with a spirit that is dead:
you come in clean robes that clothe a rotten heart;
you sing for joy as you drag your feet;
you pray practiced prayers while your mind wanders;
your spirit wants forgiveness though your flesh breeds contempt;
you request that He gives you a life, but you give only a minute.
At the sight of a lamb offered with hands stained of blood,
His heart grows weary.

"yet you do not know what tomorrow will bring. What is your life? For you are a mist that appears for a little time and then vanishes."

Remind me of my own significant insignificance.
By this I am drawn to need more than myself—
to serve more than myself,
to love more than myself.

Psalm 86:15

"But you, O LORD, are a God merciful and gracious, slow to anger and abounding in steadfast love and faithfulness."

Unparalleled your love forever shall be,
this love so full, which gifts us grace for free;
you fill our cups until they overflow,
your generosity no limit knows.
The most steadfast of hearts these eyes have seen,
you wait with patience, never do you recede;
of faithfulness you are the perfect model,
your promises you never treat as twaddle.
Oh God, how full of mercy is your heart,
without which under sin I'd fall apart;
Divine, a selfless love without conditions,
to us you grant complete and full volition.
There is no lesser love, I believe,
that you would give, and I receive.

"Therefore he had to be made like his brothers in every respect, so that he might become a merciful and faithful high priest in the service of God, to make propitiation for the sins of his people. For because he himself has suffered when tempted, he is able to help those who are being tempted."

The only King to walk this earth
who was ever worthy
was clothed in flesh like mine.

He chose to battle that flesh—that friend of temptation,
that patron of deception,
that ally of rebellion—a fiend.

He chose to come in flesh that could feel every sensation and deprivation—
the burn of infirmity and the pang of hunger,
the delights of pleasure and the agonies of pain.

He chose to wear flesh that would know pain in the most intimate way:
hands that would feel every blow of the hammer
and flesh that would be flogged and flayed.

The only King to walk this earth
who was ever worthy
was clothed in flesh like mine.

Matthew 4:19

"And he said to them, 'Follow me, and I will make you fishers of men.'"

Puffs of white skim across the cool glass mirror
upon which sits the seasoned fisher's boat.
The catch not yet awake, he casts out
and the water shivers with the echo of ripples
as it wakes to the pleasant aroma that fills its depths.

Knowing not every line will bring a catch,
but knowing no catch will come without a line extended,
he casts again,
and waits with patient expectance
as the boat's shadow marks the time.

The sea is still,
and still is he.
Again he casts,
this time with a new lure,
for he knows, what appeals to one may not the other attract.

In due time, wizened eyes discern
the wriggling shadows beginning to emerge,
and the hand is still when it senses
a hesitant nibble.

The shadow wanders away,
but still, he is glad.
Tomorrow, he will start again.

Psalm 118:24

"This is the day that the LORD *has made; let us rejoice and be glad in it."*

It is 7:47 am in Dallas, a Sunday
that shares the same calendar space as Pentecost this year.
It is 2021 and my car is squeezing between
the orange cones that are still on LBJ
while I am also trying to swerve around the potholes
that make my car shudder every time I drive in that middle lane.

I pull back the black rusted doors revealing
the place where I will be reborn
and keep the mask over my mouth
as my black-strap sandals slap the stairs I climb
to arrive at a renovated industrial office lobby with 19 people—
all hands in the pile for the afterlife!

We shuffle to another room with an old Yamaha upright and some holy paintings
whose cascade of blue and violet strokes depict Jesus,
reminding me of how he was always dripping with love,
and Joe's trapezoid mustache runs through the routine
where I share my Jesus story
then walk up to a bathtub entombed in brown stained planks and sit
in a porcelain bowl of lukewarm water
as I pinch my nose and shut my eyes to wake up to a new life

in a room whose blasting AC freezes my soaked clothes.
In the celebration I am crowned with a wreath Kaitlyn made
from royal purple and crayon yellow flowers
and clayera japonica leaves from the bush outside my apartment
while flashes blink from someone's iPhone
and then we leave for some Snooze A.M. pancakes
only to find that they're too busy for us
so we go across the parking lot to Taco Deli instead.

And now, I am chugging a half-full glass of water
to balance out the pastor taco
that was seasoned with the Dead Sea
as my 2 friends chat with my family
and I hide behind my hand so they don't see me drink the chunky guac.

When it is time to depart, they embrace me
one by one disappearing into their cars,

until I too can leave
and sit at my desk that is piled with a blanket of papers from my philosophy class.
The warming sun pierces my eyes through the slats of the shutters,
drawing my eyes to the blue sky that is saturated with a river of clouds dripping with
love.

Psalm 39:6-7

"Surely a man goes about as a shadow!
Surely for nothing they are in turmoil; man heaps up wealth and does not know who will
gather!
And now, O LORD, for what do I wait? My hope is in you."

I once placed my hope in what was not mine—
in the fleeting things of this earth.
I chased after wisdom and wealth,
I hungered for applause and amusement,
but my broken soul failed to see
that everything I had never did belong to me.
As quickly as I breathed, the winds could change
and withdraw all that I had labored for.
So long it took for me to learn the truth:
it wasn't mine on earth, but the Lord's.

So I turn to place my hope in what eternity says is mine—
not something that can be taken
out of my old, haggard hands
for another to enjoy upon my earthly end.
I claim my rightful inheritance,
promised by God, delivered by the Son, guaranteed by the Spirit;
I claim His peace and security;
I claim His provision and counsel;
I claim His love and His joy;
all these He generously bestows to those who hope in Him.

1 Peter 2:11

"Beloved, I urge you as sojourners and exiles to abstain from the passions of the flesh,
which wage war against your soul."

Truth be told, we are but passersby,
tenants residing for a temporary time
here, on this earth, I am housed as a guest,
though, with my past, I am deserving of less.
Humility, make me know this,
and fill this heart with gratitude;
cleanse me of my pride,
correct my beliefs to show true rectitude.

We are called to live in a manner reflective
of what has been revealed through greater perspective;
so with thanks I till and labor long
whilst I share the words of a sojourner's song:
Mine this wealth is not; mine this land is not;
but still, I have what I have sought.
I wait to enter the house of my parentage,
to be in the land of my holy inheritance.

1 Peter 1:12

"God revealed to the prophets that their ministry was not for their own benefit but for yours. And now, you have heard these things from the evangelists who preached the gospel to you through the power of the Holy Spirit sent from heaven—the gospel containing wonderful mysteries that even the angels long to get a glimpse of."
**from the Passion Translation*

For this brief moment, let's not be the pitied ones.
Instead, imagine the angels' hands deeply impressed
upon a white bed of cotton as they arch their necks out to see us,
living.

They see us swerving our bikes, scraping our knees,
bleeding mortality.
They see us machinating for plans A-Z because we fear the unknown.
But really, they wish they could unknow, and need dependence as desperately as we do.
They see us admiring the human faith of Abraham and Paul.
In their minds, they wonder if they could have done the same.

They see the redeemable flaws that define us.
But what they do not see is how it feels
to have the cataracts of unbelief removed—
to feel, for the first time, the full radiance of truth.

What does it mean to see?
The angels got to witness,
but our kind got to live it.

They cannot understand how it feels to know
that even when Jesus saw us
wallowing in gold
and kneeling before chiseled gods
and gnashing our teeth with hate
and forgetting the pain of every blow he took in our place,
he said we were worth it.

And so now, we have only to overcome the doubt that we face—
the doubt of the unseeing generation.
To remember (because, unlike the angels,
we are able to forget) how much of a miracle it is.

Ephesians 5:1

"Therefore be imitators of God, as beloved children."

Dad,

Can I be strong like you—
strong enough to fight evil
and do the right thing?

Can I be smart like you—
enough to make wise decisions,
and give good advice?

Can I be good like you?
You never lie,
and you always keep your promises—
I like that.

Can I be kind like you?
It hurts to hear the people
always shouting at each other,
but you listen.
You are always forgiving me.
You are patient with me.

I want to be full of hope like you.
I think it comes from how much you love—
that's what makes people really happy.

I want to be like you.

"Not that I am speaking of being in need, for I have learned in whatever situation I am to be content. I know how to be brought low, and I know how to abound. In any and every circumstance, I have learned the secret of facing plenty and hunger, abundance and need. I can do all things through him who strengthens me."

He leaves me not in my ignorant youth,
nor when I grow old;
in times of emptiness,
He feeds both body grown frail and soul malnourished.
When the light of day is soon to die,
by His light that glows in glory
He leads me to that ever-flowing stream
to refresh my unutterably parched soul.
Though I do not claim to seek trials,
I welcome them readily,
for I know I have the Lord as my defense.

Yet I should admit, how I fear myself in times of plenty—
how much more must I rely on the Lord!
For it is my own foolish arrogance
that succumbs to the call of wealth,
whose luxuries, once tasted,
can so quickly disfigure a man uninhibited.
None but He could check the beast within;
He gives me what I need in times of trials and prosperity.

"Are not five sparrows sold for two pennies? And not one of them is forgotten before God. Why, even the hairs of your head are all numbered. Fear not; you are of more value than many sparrows."

As He painted every feather of every sparrow,
and as a creator loves every inch of his work,
so too does He treasure every hair of your head
which He sculpted from the clays of the earth.

Yet still, you are flightier than the sparrow
who sings with a fearless joy;
how long will its song outlast human breath
which breathes fear of man before God?

"For we do not wrestle against flesh and blood, but against the rulers, against the authorities, against the cosmic powers over this present darkness, against the spiritual forces of evil in the heavenly places. Therefore take up the whole armor of God, that you may be able to withstand in the evil day, and having done all, to stand firm. Stand therefore, having fastened on the belt of truth, and having put on the breastplate of righteousness, and, as shoes for your feet, having put on the readiness given by the gospel of peace. In all circumstances take up the shield of faith, with which you can extinguish all the flaming darts of the evil one; and take the helmet of salvation, and the sword of the Spirit, which is the word of God,"

Saints! Hear your call to arms in this war of spirits—
today and every day we stand against those evil forces
who crawl forth from a place of darkness,
who answer to the spiteful prince of rebellion.
Daily don the armor you have been given
and receive the strength of the Lord of Hosts.
Hold fast to those tools of truth and discernment,
that you may not be ensnared by the enemies' traps;
put on your breastplates and beat them boldly—
let our enemies tremble at our thundering confidence
from having followed Christs' righteous ways;
run with all swiftness to spread the news to the people:
our King has already defeated the enemy!

You shall face a constant battery of fire—
though some days will burn greater than others—
but hold up your shield that is your faith
and steadily you shall advance in every circumstance.
Indeed, our most vulnerable head and heart
are fiercely guarded by our salvation which cannot be denied.
Let the Lord of Armies mark our breasts and crowns
with the crest of His salvation;
we are His saints, now and forever!

"until we all attain to the unity of the faith and of the knowledge of the Son of God, to mature manhood, to the measure of the stature of the fullness of Christ, so that we may no longer be children, tossed to and fro by the waves and carried about by every wind of doctrine, by human cunning, by craftiness in deceitful schemes."

In the row of shops and wooden stalls, craftsmen call to the crowds passing through. A gaunt man in black with a gentleman's top hat offers his wares. A young girl is drawn in by his hands that beckon toward a jar that's labeled as, "MATURITY." In ordinary letters below: "Directions for Use: Sit and wait until you are older. Then swallow one pill, and you will be mature."

"It's free," he says, and her eyes widen with her smile. Oblivious in her excitement, she hastens home whilst scheming hands peel off an aged guise. He claps with ungodly glee while chanting, "Of many things does age pretend to know, but the girl trades precious time for false maturity. Idly she'll wait and spend her years, all the while learning nothing. Oh, how Elihu would be dismayed!"

"to put off your old self, which belongs to your former manner of life and is corrupt through deceitful desires,"

Some days, on those still days,
where the lull of idleness tempts me to reminisce,
I pull out from the closet a big brown box
filled with my old clothes.

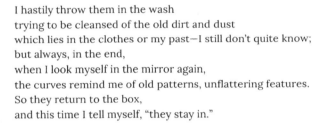

Sometimes, I am strong,
and I smile—grateful, that the past is the past—
then close the box, and move on.
But sometimes, I slip them on—"just for a minute" I say—
and I slip easily into earlier ways.

I hastily throw them in the wash
trying to be cleansed of the old dirt and dust
which lies in the clothes or my past—I still don't quite know;
but always, in the end,
when I look myself in the mirror again,
the curves remind me of old patterns, unflattering features.
So they return to the box,
and this time I tell myself, "they stay in."

Ecclesiastes 7:2

"It is better to go to the house of mourning than to go to the house of feasting,
for this is the end of all mankind, and the living will lay it to heart."

Even before turning onto the street, one can hear mouth-stuffed
chatter and the metallic clanking of cups,
cheers and raucous laughter and the music of fiddles.
It is a grand golden house with bright lights and several floors,
With visitors seated around long tables in the front rooms by the door
and residents housed in the back,
servers milling about with food and drink in a never-ending feast where all is at ease—
no cares must be carried
and no pains must hurt
when they can be drowned out by the business and cast onto the dirty floor.
Forgotten.
Hungry hands grab everything the eyes take in
and before he can lean back to enjoy the scene
another plate is set before him,
prompting him to pick at the meat 'til he reaches
bone.
Restless, he moves deeper into the maze of a house
with its endless chambers of splendor to get lost in;
but as he goes further, the windows disappear and the smoky haze of turkeys and
hams
leads to rooms filled with sitting figures with heavy lids and drunken tongues
whose sleep is never restful
because the crowded space never quiets
and there is no room for silence.

Across the street is a dreary looking path that seems well-worn, yet empty,
with a somber little cottage at the end.
New visitors dread the foreboding walk,
but returners know there is a warm fire and fellowship waiting.
Inside, laughter and silence create a steady cadence of remembrance.
Stories are passed around to be added onto by old and new friends.
Words that were held close are spoken and shared
to breathe new life into aging memories.
Sorrow and suffering
and love and affection tread their tongues.
When conversation slows, the silence does not feel heavy—more like a comforter,
a blanket wrapped around this circle of people who remember,
"Our time here is short, and here is someone who filled it well."
They are made to remember their smallness in a crowded world;

but the single room filled with figures huddled together
reminds them of how full that smallness can be.

The fire casts its light on each face in the circle,
appreciating every presence.
Some have been there for days. Some will only stay a few hours.
But for all of them, the walk back home will not feel so lonely.

"And he said to him, 'You shall love the LORD your God with all your heart and with all your soul and with all your mind. This is the great and first commandment. And a second is like it: You shall love your neighbor as yourself.'"

Dearest,
I thought of you today.
It was once commanded,
"You shall love your neighbor as yourself."
I have known many to struggle with the first bit,
but I know you lean toward neglecting the latter;
you do not love others as yourself,
but as much, much more.
Would I be glad at so selfless a thing,
had I not seen on so many an occasion
how it is done as a detriment to your self.
Against this I urge you,
to not undervalue your worth (and I say this in full confidence
that you are not one to overvalue it),
for it is that love which is to be
the reference of measurement for all others.
Are you not held in high regard
by the Lord who gave you life?
As one of His, do not discount yourself
as any less loved than those others.

"Whoever does not bear his own cross and come after me cannot be my disciple. For which of you, desiring to build a tower, does not first sit down and count the cost, whether he has enough to complete it?. . . . So therefore, any one of you who does not renounce all that he has cannot be my disciple."

"Is this the radical love I hear them speak of,
that even when I forego all the other kinds,
His one is more than enough
to sooth my poor heart?
To undo the ties of my desires that make me
like a puppet on strings, I'll give everything!
Take my excess and no longer
will I have the choicest foods to appease my weak body
or the chance to adorn myself in many rich robes."

"Oh Heart! Where does your loyalty lie?
Should the leveling floods come and take all away,
would you turn from this love to chase after fleeting things?
Around what are the veins of your heart
still wrapped and drawing false life from?"

"Spirit, what more do I have that I can give?
I want to know Him.
My ambitions, I grant, are frequently foiled,
so I count it not too great a loss.
Time I have, but it is limited and therefore precious,
as is my life here on this earth—
God gave me this life, did He not?"

"Truly, He was the one.
But I would caution you to remember:
your time in this place is but a phase
before you ascend to that heavenly place.
How will you pass it?"

"If I am a pilgrim,
take my house of bricks and mortar then,
and I shall follow where He leads
so I can learn what I truly need to survive.

"You are ready to surrender to uncertainty,
but is there not more space for vulnerability?"

"You ask for my pride.
I suppose if it means
I'll have less room to fall,
take also my fear!
I should like to be free of that."

"And what keeps your fear beating?"

"The acceptance of men leaves me restless—
it never stays for long
no matter how much I try to secure it.
But it is all that is left for me."

"Ah, but what about His love
which is abundant and overflows—
the very thing you first sought?"

"I had forgotten
it is enough.
If it is these things He asks for,
and everything He gives,
take my pride and pleasure, those elusive things
that ebb and flow with the tides of circumstance
and the fickle approval of men.
I'll trade it for comfort,
the enduring comfort that only Jesus can bring."

Psalm 150:6

"Let everything that has breath praise the LORD!
Praise the LORD!*"*

Standing still with my feet planted in flowering grass
as I look not only forward, but around,
my own distinctness melts away
into the body of Creation
to stand with trees whose fingers reach toward heaven.

There is a hidden song
in the crescendo of a rising sun that calls forth the day,
in the songs of the birds and the song of the breeze
that twirls through my hair and flutters staccato leaves.
A giddy laugh bubbles up from my throat
and the twisting grass directs my steps
in a carefree dance that is both chaotic and lovely.
Above, light-filled clouds invoke the o-shaped sound of singing angels
to match the lively beat of dragonfly wings next to me.
My soul cries to rise "Up, up, up!"

There is a hidden song
in the soft chorus of night's blooming pansy sky,
in the bass humming of mountains
that invites a musical silence
from all living creatures
as soul attaches to ascending song
and yearns to sing with the voices of heaven, "holy, holy, holy!"

John 15:9-11

"As the Father has loved me, so have I loved you. Abide in my love. If you keep my commandments, you will abide in my love, just as I have kept my Father's commandments and abide in his love. These things I have spoken to you, that my joy may be in you, and that your joy may be full."

A voice in my head told me
my heart needed cleaning today,
so I sat down and looked
at its many shelves and
hidden compartments.

Atop the first shelf was a jar of gold.
Then there were various trophies and accolades,
books with scholarly authorities,
and dreams sculpted by my own hands.

But then, at the very bottom, tucked
away in the corner of my heart,
there was a beaded chain
with an anchor at the end. I pulled it,
and a trap door gave way
to a starved spirit.
At first,
it seemed I was looking upon a stranger,
and it frightened me
that my heart would house such a foreign thing.
But, once I looked
past the gaunt bones and weary brow,
He seemed to flicker,
as if some innate light in Him started at my recognition.
At once I felt my mind feeding me
memories of forgotten pains that had once
been salved by this tender spirit
who had nursed so faithfully the cuts
of my tears and wounds inflicted
by the wicked voices of loneliness.

This Spirit, who had been so sturdy and sure,
had been pushed further
and further
down in my heart
until He sank

to the very bottom. I had deposed Him.

I wept at my villainy
and the more I wept,
the more the shelves of my heart shook
and snapped and crumbled to dust
leaving the jar and the letters and the trophies and the books and the sculptures
nowhere to stand and so
they fell
and shattered when they met the ground
and melted into dust.
And this, I will admit, increased the current
of the wailing river in my soul,
for I would have nothing left to love,
and what is life without that highest purpose?

When finally the flow of my tears
had run its course,
I noticed a small movement
and once more looked into my heart.

There He was,
standing so strong and sure
with eyes looking up at me,
so gentle and knowing.
He had grown now to fill
the space that had once been divided.
The light which had been only a glint
was now a glorious and nourishing glow
that had already begun
to heal the cracked walls of my shabby heart
that I had never noticed before.
His mouth opened with a red fire
that sounded like the voice I had heard;
it caught at the edges of ashen piles
from the idols that had fallen,
and my heart was made clean.

I made for Him a bed to stay
and He brought with Him a lamp.
Through bleary eyes
I smiled at Him,
and He smiled at me.

Writing Your Own Meditative Poems

Lectio Divina

What is Lectio Divina?

Lectio Divina, or "divine reading," is a monastic method of prayer that helps provide spiritual insight. It focuses on repeating recitations of scripture and opening up conversation with God through prayer.

How can I practice Lectio Divina with poetry?

Writing poems is a valuable practice that can help reveal the richness of the Word. The act of repeatedly reading the same portion of scripture allows the words to soak into our minds and hearts, and this meditation can help revive our understanding of the text in new and refreshing ways. Here are some simple steps you can take to practice writing your own meditative poems:

1. **Grab your Bible.** Find a quiet place that is free of distractions so you can focus in on what God is revealing to you through His Word.

2. **Pray.** Invite Him to help you understand what you are about to read.

3. **Read.** Choose a passage to read. For writing poems, I usually stay within one chapter to encourage a slow, thoughtful reading pace. As you go through a passage, listen for a word or phrase that grabs your attention. For me, this can involve a word that seems out of place, a scene that is vividly described, a message that convicts me, or one that makes me feel overwhelmed by God's goodness in the best way. Savor it.

4. **Read again.** This time, think about *how* your heart is moved. What images or phrases come to mind that are especially gripping? What is so striking about that passage? Are you seeing a familiar passage from a new angle?

5. **Reflect.** Use your imagination and think of all the nuanced meanings of that word or phrase that struck you. Begin to jot all those thoughts down as you continue to meditate on that portion of scripture. Choose one idea that you want to run with or look for a thematic idea that runs through your notes and begin to weave that into your poem. Your poem can simply be descriptive, or it can tell a story. Whatever direction you feel prompted to take, consider your poem a form of worship.

   If you're unsure of where to start, it's okay to pause. When I read scripture, I don't sit down with the intention of writing a poem. Rather, I try and immerse myself in the story to understand what it reveals about God, and if a thought is particularly moving to me, I'll begin writing phrases or images I want to remember. Sometimes it helps to take a step away to let your ideas marinate. Come back to your notes a few days later with fresh eyes. As you write, continue to ask what ideas God is inviting you to explore. If you feel your poem is going in a strange direction, check to see if it aligns with scripture, which is a source of God's revelations to humanity.

Made in the USA
Coppell, TX
01 July 2023

18655299R00036